The Late and Clever Mr Green

Gardener to Sir George Macleay at Pendell Court

JAMES DRIVER

Copyright © James Driver 2016

All rights reserved. No part of this publication may be reproduced or transmitted in any form or by any means, electronic or mechanical including photocopying, recording or any information storage or retrieval system, without prior permission in writing from the publishers.

The moral rights of the author have been asserted

First published in the United Kingdom in 2016
by
The Cloister House Press

ISBN 978-1-909465-45-9

*'Of man's first disobedience, and the fruit
Of that forbidden tree, whose mortal taste
Brought death into the world, and all our woe,
With loss of Eden...'*

THE LATE AND CLEVER MR GREEN

In the first week of March, 1882, Charles Green, the quiet, self-effacing, Head Gardener at Pendell Court, Bletchingley, the Surrey home of Sir George Macleay, carefully opened the latest edition of *The Gardener's Chronicle*. Filling the whole of page 303 was an accurately rendered, if rather pedestrian, wood engraving of a plant he had first bred some seven years earlier. It was named after him: *Streptocarpus greenii*. A short paragraph on the preceding page gave the *Chronicle's* readers a simplified, but still useful, practical explanation of how to grow Green's hybrid: the first successful *Streptocarpus* cross ever recorded.

The *Chronicle* enjoyed an international reputation for authoritative accuracy on all matters horticultural, and was read avidly across the English-speaking world by professional and amateur gardeners alike. To be featured in it by name was to be singled out, in a highly competitive field, as one of the best.

Charles Green was no stranger to its pages. His first appearance had come ten years earlier, in 1872, when he was Head Gardener at Hillfield, the famous Reigate garden of William Wilson Saunders.

'...and when we state, as we can truly, that the whole establishment is in excellent order, we pay no empty or unmeaning compliment to the zeal and skill of the gardener, Mr Green.'

Six years later, in 1878, *The Gardener's Chronicle* ran its first feature on Green's work at Pendell Court. *The Garden,* a rival to the *Chronicle* edited by the influential garden theorist William Robinson, followed suit in both 1881 and 1882. In 1883 the first edition of Robinson's book *'The English Flower Garden'* praised the gardens at Pendell Court as an exemplar of *'...what was best in the way of design or style...'*

But within eighteen months of its publication, at the height of his fame, and enjoying the kind of success and public recognition that most Victorian gardeners could only dream about, Charles Green forsook the remarkable gardens he had created at Pendell Court. Shortly afterwards he retreated to a small terraced house in Reigate. It was here, just two doors along from where his beloved daughter was raising his five young grandchildren, he drank himself to death.

Charles's Green's third and final master, Sir George Macleay, died less than five years later, on June 24th 1891, at the Chalet des Rosiers at Mentone on the French Riviera. His last day in England had been November 19th 1890 when he had sailed for France with his new wife, Lady Augusta. They had been married in January 1890 when Sir George was eighty-one and his bride was fifty-two. Augusta was Sir George's second wife; his first wife, Barbara, had died in 1869.

The wedding had taken place at Totteridge parish church in Hertfordshire, next door to Totteridge Grange, the home of one of Sir George's oldest friends, Sir Charles Nicholson. Both men had made their fortunes in Australia and both retained a keen interest in its colonies. The Australian newspapers, however, were not impressed. The *Wagga Wagga Advertiser* informed its readers, not entirely truthfully:

'Sir George Macleay was married yesterday to Miss Sams of Hobart. She is of mature years, and has for some time been his housekeeper.'

The Chalet des Rosiers was one of the most fashionable villas for rent on the French Riviera. In 1882 it had been the venue for Queen Victoria's most successful foreign holiday. Sir George could afford his prolonged stay. On his death his personal estate was valued at around £70,000: the equivalent today of a fortune somewhere in the region of £7,000,000.

Mentone was an obvious choice as a winter resort for the Macleays. Not only was it highly fashionable with its grand hotels, promenades and casino, but its extremely mild climate enabled all manner of sub-tropical plants to flourish. Sir George could enjoy strolling and driving in the open air among plants that at Pendell Court could only flourish under glass.

Before Sir George died Lady Augusta had made a point of insisting that he did not leave her Pendell Court in his will. Her lack of sympathy for the house, the gardens, and her husband's loyal servants, was reflected in the sensational court case that made headlines in the national newspapers in June 1893. One of her domestic servants, Catherine Aberdeen, the niece of Sir George's actual housekeeper, Barbara Gunn, accused her mistress of libel. Following an acrimonious dispute between Lady Augusta and Miss Aberdeen over the latter's future,

Sir George's widow had written to Miss Aberdeen's aunt accusing her niece of drinking to excess and being pregnant through an illicit affair with a footman named Jacques. Through a legal technicality the court found in favour of Lady Augusta and Catherine Aberdeen was forced to pay the costs.

It is hard to imagine such a situation arising when Sir George was alive. Macleay was a kind-hearted employer, a well-liked Lord of the Manor and a generous benefactor to those in need. In his will he left Barbara Gunn, his real housekeeper, the huge sum of £1000; this in an era when she might expect an annual wage of around £70. His annual 'treats' in the 1880s for the inmates of the local workhouse – the Godstone Union – with piles of cakes for the children, tobacco and pipes for the men and 'gin toddy' all round, were legendary.

For Macleay the belief of Sir Francis Bacon that *'Money is like muck, not good except it be spread'* was a self-evident truth, particularly when applied to Pendell Court. At the heart of the enigmatic tale of Charles Green and Sir George Macleay is the dramatic rise, and equally sudden fall, of this great Victorian garden: one that flourished for barely fifteen years before disappearing almost without trace.

❁   ❁   ❁

George Macleay (1809-1891) first came to prominence through his involvement in Charles Sturt's explorations in 1829-30 along the Murrumbidgee and Murray rivers. His role in the expedition '...*as a companion than an assistant...*' brought him fame, fortune and carved for him a seemingly indestructible niche in Australian history. Although it was the only such journey he ever undertook, over 60 years later his obituaries still remembered him as: *'explorer'*.

Before federation the individual colonies that made up Australia were all governed independently, and each had its own governor and legislative councils. George's father, Alexander Macleay (1767-1848), had been appointed Colonial Secretary for New South Wales in 1825. He had arrived in Sydney in 1826. His son, who was expelled from Westminster School in London in 1827, followed close behind.

It was probably something of a relief for the beleaguered Alexander – colonial politics in the 1830s were a notoriously cut-throat affair and he was soon working twelve hours a day to try and exert some sort of control on the burgeoning colony's affairs – when, in 1829, one of Sturt's original party dropped out at the last minute and he was able to suggest his gregarious, affable, enthusiastic, energetic and wholly optimistic 20 year old son as a substitute.

The rigours of the journey permanently damaged the health of Charles Sturt (1795-1869). For a time he went almost completely blind and it was not until 1834 that he received a grant of 5,000 acres of land in recognition of his labours. Macleay, no doubt helped by his family connections, received his 2,500 acres far more promptly and by 1831 had embarked on the farming career that was to form the basis of his considerable fortune.

In 1826, the same year that Charles Green (1826-1886) was born, William Gardner Sams (1792-1871) arrived in Hobart, Tasmania, on board the ship *'Harvey'* commanded by a Captain Peach. Like George Macleay he came from a privileged background but, again like Macleay, one that couldn't offer him enough of a private income to flourish in Great Britain. His father had held a post in the Royal Household and William had been for a time a page in the service of the Duke of Kent, the father of Queen Victoria. On his arrival in Tasmania he was given a generous grant of land, but failed to make a success of farming and took up instead the post of Commissioner of the Insolvent Court.

After falling out with the notoriously autocratic Sir George Arthur, the Governor of Tasmania – or Van Diemen's Land as it was known then – Sams was made redundant. Furious at his treatment he took the arduous three or four month journey *back* to England so that he could appeal in person to the King. William IV, who had briefly met Sams when younger, listened to what he had to say and re-instated him. Sams returned to Tasmania something of a hero. He continued his role at the Insolvency Court and undertook various other legal duties until he was pensioned off in 1863. His youngest daughter, Augusta, was born in 1838.

There is a slightly disparaging reference to Augusta in a newspaper report of her father's death in 1871.

'His youngest daughter resided there with him, and on Friday last, in reply to an enquiry about her

father's health, said he appeared quite well. Next day he died'.

Augusta Sams (1838-1919) was 33 and unmarried when William died. Her mother had died two years earlier and it is likely that Augusta would have been expected to run her elderly father's house. He was 70 when he passed away. As is the case for many women in the 19th century who were prevented by the circumstances of their birth and class from living independently, or following a career or course of their own choosing, it is difficult to discover much more about Augusta's early life except that by December 1871 she was requesting that the Tasmanian authorities pay her the arrears of pension due to her late father. They agreed, and she received the sum of £84 13 shillings and fourpence.

If the circumstances of Augusta Sams' life make it difficult to discover much about how she lived, then those of two sisters born to a bricklayer in rural early nineteenth century England make them almost invisible. The two wives of Charles Green, Emily (1827-1919) and Lucy Rowland (1828-1858), were baptised in Shipley Church, Sussex, in 1827 and

1828 respectively. Shipley is a Sussex village about 30 miles by road from Lewes.

The late 1820s were hard years for the rural population of Great Britain. A series of poor harvests in 1828, 1829 and 1830 coincided with radical changes in farming methods, large scale enclosure of common land, a surplus of labourers and the economic recession that followed the boom years of the Napoleonic Wars. The wages of agricultural labourers dropped and crime in rural areas, especially poaching and stealing food, increased by 30% between 1824 and 1830. The most likely records to remain of those living, like the Rowlands, on the edge of poverty would be criminal ones. The 'Swing' riots of 1830 resulted in over a thousand people being imprisoned or transported to Australia for life. They were known as the Convict Settlers and provided a handy pool of labour for the Free Settlers like the Sams, the Sturts, the Innes and the Macleays to draw upon.

Between 1830 and 1840 the key to making a fortune as a Free Settler in Australia, was land. Unlike his father, who exhausted his resources building a fashionable house and accompanying gardens in Sydney, or his future brother-in-law,

Archibald Innes, who was eventually ruined through his lavish hospitality and acts of generosity towards both friends and strangers, George Macleay carefully and steadily first accumulated, and then turned a profit on, a great many acres. For a young man totally inexperienced in either farming or commerce, it was a remarkable achievement.

George Macleay began his career as a 'pastoralist' at Brownlow Hill, a farm belonging to his father and which, to begin with, he worked jointly with his younger brother James. On his return from Sturt's expedition he devoted himself not only to the farm, but also to establishing a fine garden. He asked his sister Fanny to send him gardening books from Sydney. He requested, and was sent, cuttings from the same city's Botanic Gardens. By the age of twenty-seven he had discovered the passion that, almost fifty years later, was to reach its spectacular climax at Pendell Court.

Macleay's most valued book in these early days was one of the key self-help books of the early 19th century: Loudon's *'An Encyclopedia of Gardening comprising the theory and practice of Horticulture, Floriculture...and Landscape Gardening.'* It was first published in 1822. Loudon also wrote on agriculture, natural history, architecture, founded magazines, designed cemeteries and an arboretum, developed ideas for greenhouse design and compiled the *'Arboretum et Fruticeum Britannicum'* – a bold attempt to record all the shrubs and trees growing in Britain.

William Borrer (1781-1862), Charles Green's first employer, had generously contributed a vast amount of material to this latter project, most of it relating to the willow family. In the 1844, posthumous, edition Loudon gave a list of the 81 different species of *Salix* that were growing in Borrer's gardens at Barrow Hill in Henfield, the house that his father had built for him on the occasion of his marriage in 1810. It is possible that Loudon and Green may have met there, although Loudon died aged sixty in 1843 when Green was only seventeen.

'The Encyclopedia of Gardening' was as comprehensive a guide as any young gardener could have wished for, and was illustrated throughout. It encompassed everything: the history of gardens from Eden to the 1820s, how to classify plants, a detailed anatomy of plants, how to use different manures, the

construction of hot houses, how to design gardens, how to dig gardens, making vegetable gardens, making flower gardens, nursery gardens, how to landscape gardens…the headings march on endlessly through more than a thousand pages and much of the practical content could be as applied as usefully today as it was almost 200 years ago

The final sections that include – *'Of the different Conditions of Men engaged in the Practice or Pursuit of Gardening'* and *'Of the education of gardeners'* reveal most vividly the nuances of the world in which Green worked, and how he didn't always follow its accepted paths.

'The knowledge of languages, history, geography, arts, sciences and literature, which a gardener daily occupied with his profession may acquire, provided he begins at the commencement of his apprenticeship, and continues to employ his leisure hours in reading till he is twenty or twenty-five years of age, is by no means inconsiderable: not that he can, or need become learned, but, if desirous, may become generally intelligent; render himself fit, as far as conversation is concerned, for good society…and provide a reserve fund of enjoyment for

himself, by laying up a store of ideas for reflection in misfortune, disease, or old age.'

'Journeyman. The period of a journeyman ought to continue till the man is at least 25 years of age. During this period he ought not to remain above one year in any situation....he ought first to engage himself a year in a public botanic garden; the next year in a public nursery...he should again enter a private garden and continue making yearly changes in the most eminent of this class of gardens, till he meets with a situation as a head gardener.'

'Botanic gardeners...Botanic gardeners also collect and dry specimens of plants, and also of mosses, fungi, algae...to this they often join the collecting of insects, birds and other animals.'

'Proprietors of gardens, who are the most eminent of all patrons, promoting every department of the art and employing serving, tradesmen and artist gardeners. A man whose garden is his own for ever, or for a considerable length of time, whether that garden be surrounded by a fence of a few hundred feet, or a park wall of ten or twelve miles,

will always be effecting some change in arrangement, or culture, favorable to trade and to artists.'

'Whatever theory therefore the young gardener may adopt, there is only one practice which he will find to answer his expectations; and that is, the strictest regard to truth, honesty, sobriety, decency, and purity in himself...'

Hardly anything is known about Charles Green before 1841 when, aged 15, he is first recorded as working as a gardener for William Borrer, except that he was born in Lewes, Sussex, in 1826 and his father's name was Francis. It has been estimated that, in 1841, out of a United Kingdom population of around 27,000,000 over 1,000,000 were employed as domestic servants – a category that included gardeners. The only category that exceeded this was that of agricultural labourers.

The extent to which the moneyed classes relied on servants in the 19th century is neatly illustrated by a set of inscriptions at Westminster School in London. It became a tradition in the early part of the nineteenth century for pupils to commemorate their time at the school by literally leaving their mark, usually their name and an accompanying date, inscribed in the stonework of the School Gateway, also known as Burlington's Arch. George Macleay's name is there, dated 1826, as are those of two of his brothers. None of these carvings, however, were executed by any of the Macleays. They are all the work of professional stonemasons, hired for the purpose by the young gentlemen from among those working at Westminster Abbey which adjoins the school.

It is misleading to think that such clear divisions as this between the accepted roles of master and servant prevented the latter from being able to join the ranks of the former. The most cited example for gardeners was Joseph Paxton (1803-1865), who rose from garden boy to Member of Parliament; finding time on his journey to be Head Gardener at Chatsworth, design the Crystal Palace, be knighted by Queen Victoria, and help found *The Gardener's Chronicle.* William Robinson (1838-1935), founder of the rival magazine, *The Garden,* also started as a garden boy and was so accomplished by the age of 29 that his election as fellow of the Linnean Society in 1866 was sponsored, amongst others, by Charles

Darwin. By 1884 Robinson's writing on matters horticultural had been so successful he was able to buy Gravetye Manor in Sussex and employ gardeners and agricultural labourers of his own to tend its 200 acres.

Stories like these were told and recorded because they were unusual. Personal advancement on such a scale almost always required the intervention at some early stage of a benevolent employer. Charles Green was lucky enough to find just such a man at the very start of his career – the Sussex botanist William Borrer.

There is very little precise evidence as to exactly what Green's roles were during the twenty or more years he worked for Borrer. There is the occasional record of events that he was likely to have witnessed. For example, towards the start of his time at Barrow Hill, when Green was aged just 15, The *Brighton Gazette* for July 22nd 1841 reported:

'Dr Forster, the astronomer and meteorologist, who has been making the geological tour of Great Britain, has traced the late thunderstorm across the island. It began at Brighton, fell heavily in parts of Sussex, destroying in one conservatory alone, at

Henfield (Mr Borrer's), 3,000 panes of glass, the hailstones falling of the size of eggs;'

But after 150 years, and with no mention of him in Borrer's surviving correspondence, and no sign of any surviving diaries or any other personal memoranda of Green from this time, it remains impossible to recover precisely what he thought, or to give reasons as to why he acted in a particular way. All that can be known for sure is a little about the world in which he grew up, and nothing of how he perceived it.

This is very different to what is known about the scientific elite of the 19th century. Although the minutiae of their disputes and theories can sometimes be confusing, it is easy to unearth what they thought, wrote and said, simply because of the wealth of original material that has been preserved. The societies to which they belonged kept detailed minutes of their proceedings. Their speeches and debates were often reported in popular newspapers, they preserved each other's correspondence, they wrote books, presented scientific papers – many of which were later printed – they were gossiped about, they kept journals and diaries, were quoted and discussed in their colleagues' memoirs and after their deaths their personal papers were often deposited in museum or university archives.

A keen amateur interest in many branches of natural history – most particularly zoology and horticulture – was a constant thread running through George Macleay's life. His father was a passionate amateur naturalist and before going to Australia had amassed one of the world's greatest collections of insects. In 1836, at the age of 29, George had been appointed to the committee of the Australian Museum and Botanical Garden. On his return to England in 1860 he was elected to the Linnean Society of London, an exclusive club for gentlemen scientists. He became a member of its council in 1864. George Macleay mixed socially with many of the most eminent scientists of his day. Among these was Sir Richard Owen (1804-1892). Chiefly remembered today as the inventor of the term *'dinosaur'*, and for his determined campaigning that led eventually to the foundation of the Natural History Museum in London, Richard Owen was regarded by many of his contemporaries as a gifted scientist, but also an unstable and often rabid opponent.

Owen's feuds were legendary. In 1848 he was criticized at a meeting of the Royal Society by the palaeontologist Gideon Mantell (1790-1852). Mantell not only questioned Owen's scientific methodology, but also addressed what he saw as Owen's blatant plagiarism. Not surprisingly Owen was furious at being verbally attacked in public - and in front of his peers - and for the next four years did his best to belittle all of Mantell's ground-breaking research on fossil creatures. As others had found out to their cost, facing up to Owen meant one had to be prepared to withstand all manner of spite and bitterness. He excelled himself with Mantell. When the latter died in 1852, Owen somehow obtained a section of his rival's deformed spine, preserved it in a specimen jar and then presented it to the Royal College of Surgeons.

Remarkably Macleay never seemed to quarrel with any of his fellow scientists. In the 1870s, at the same time he was helping Owen with a book on Australian fossils – for which he received fulsome praise from the author – he arranged for a splendid specimen of *Ceratodus,* a lungfish, to be sent especially from Australia for Thomas Huxley to study. Huxley and Owen had been bitter enemies since they had clashed over Darwin's views on evolution.

❀ ❀ ❀

William Borrer's life and work offer a more civilised example of how the gentlemen scientists of the early and mid-nineteenth century were able to make so much progress, so quickly, in so many areas of specialist research. With a healthy private income that left him untroubled by financial matters or the necessity to work for a living, and with all domestic duties being fulfilled by teams of both indoor and outdoor staff, Borrer was free to pursue whatever course of study he wished. With no desire, or need, for personal advancement he was content to see his research used in the books and papers of others. Twenty-one species of native British plants were first recorded by him, and he also discovered an impressive number of new lichens and ferns.

Borrer embraced any new technology that would help him in his studies. As the railway network spread rapidly across Britain he made a point of taking long train journeys to check reported sightings of new plants or to explore likely locations. As he travelled he kept a keen eye out the window for any unusual flora growing by the side of the track. If he thought he spotted something, he would alight from the train at the next station and walk back beside the rails until he was able to identify what he had seen.

Outside of his membership of the usual scientific societies – he was elected to the Linnean Society in 1805, aged only 24 – Borrer showed no interest in pursuing any sort of career in public life. He did, however, take a keen interest in Henfield, the small Sussex town where he lived. As well as making generous financial donations to the local church, he was instrumental in setting up an Infant School in 1844, ran a Sunday School in his own house for his neighbours' children, and seems to have taken a personal interest in the education of various promising individuals. Whatever it was that made him realise it would be worth encouraging the young Charles Green is unrecorded, as are Green's reasons for beginning his career in Henfield. What is certain is that the two men struck up a rapport that lasted over twenty years until Borrer's death in 1862.

The usual course of an ambitious gardener's career was to spend his formative years in one place as an apprentice, then to move through a variety of jobs gaining experience as a journeyman in as many different areas of horticulture as possible, before applying for a first post as Head Gardener. Charles Green simply stayed with Borrer for more than two decades, devoting all his energies to the gardens at Barrow Hill. Judging by his later career it seems that it was Borrer's extensive range of heated greenhouses and their collections of orchids and exotic, foreign, plants that captured the young gardener's imagination.

The impressions Green left on others, although far fewer than the numerous records of Macleay, reveal a man of marked sensibilities. The *Sussex Express* of September 19th 1857 gives two glimpses of his artistry and skill at raising and nurturing unusual plants. Green was now aged 31, and still with Borrer. They appear in the paper's report of the Brighton and Sussex Floricultural and Horticultural Show held at the Royal Pavilion.

'A most splendid and rare collection of exotic grasses exhibited by Mr Charles Green, gardener to Wm. Borrer esq. of Henfield. They were as graceful as they were choice, and were admired by all.'

'...a miniature rock work and fernery...It was built on a square stand and ... covered with a large

bell jar. It contained 30 species of ferns in the most healthy state, many of the ferns being as rare as they were handsome.'

Charles Green won a special prize for the latter. He proudly brought it home to show his first wife, Lucy, who was pregnant with their daughter.

David Rowland, the bricklayer father of Emily and Lucy Rowland, died, aged 50, in 1845. He and his wife, also called Lucy, and his two daughters, had moved a few miles from Shipley to West Grinstead. On the death of her husband the elder Lucy moved her family again, this time a little further along the road to Henfield. To earn enough to live on they set themselves up as dressmakers.

Charles Green may have first seen the younger Lucy Rowland at St. Peter's Church in Henfield. Their long working hours would have left them little time for socialising on any day but Sunday, and William Borrer's unwavering belief in the importance of a leading a Christian life would probably have influenced his favourite gardener's religious observance too. Church-going, with its opportunities for sitting quietly and observing carefully the other members of the congregation, socialising in the churchyard afterwards and the slow walk home, were accepted times for respectable courting. Charles and Lucy were certainly married at St. Peter's, on 12th November 1856. The bride was aged 28, the groom was 30 – both slightly older than the average couple.

Their life together was short. Lucy died, probably during, or very soon after, giving birth to their only child, also christened Lucy, in 1858. As was commonplace in the mid-19th century, her unmarried sister, Emily and her mother – the elder Lucy – moved in to look after the baby and to housekeep for Charles.

No written description or image of any kind exists of Lucy Green. No gravestone remains in Henfield churchyard. The first wife of Sir George Macleay, Barbara St. Clair Innes, was commemorated after her death in 1869 by a marble sculpture in the Macleay Chapel in Godstone Church in Surrey. It is an extraordinary piece of work that like much mid-Victorian Art asks questions of its audience. Barbara Macleay reclines on a bed – or is it a chaise longue? She is dressed either in an elaborate nightgown – or perhaps she is already in her shroud? She looks towards the onlooker – or are her sightless eyes closing as Death has already claimed her? The flowers she holds appear to be slipping from her grasp.

The sculptor Macleay commissioned to carry out the work was Charles Summers. He too had recently returned from Australia where his monument to the explorers Burke and Wills – the first sculpture ever cast in bronze in Australia – had been unveiled to great acclaim. Macleay himself is often cited as an intriguing footnote in the history of Victorian sculpture. In 1852 Thomas Woolner, a founder member of the Pre-Raphaelite Brotherhood, had emigrated to Australia to seek his fortune in the goldfields. When that enterprise failed he turned to making plaster portrait miniatures of Australian high society. Among the thirty who sat for him were Charles Nicholson and George Macleay. On his return to England in 1854 Woolner had his plaster models cast in bronze. Examples of all thirty finished portraits have been identified, except for four: one of which is George Macleay's.

Barbara Macleay was 61 when she died. She had married George in 1842 when she was 34 and he was 33. They had no children. She was the sister of

Archibald Innes who had married George's elder sister Margaret. Much like the aristocracy in Great Britain, the wealthiest settlers in Australia often intermarried and so strengthened their hold on property and power. A characteristic note written by her when she was in London in 1863 still survives. It is to Sir William Macarthur, another Australian landowner.

'5, Seamore Place, Mayfair
My Dear Sir William,
I am going to ask you to receive two tiny presents from me – one a small book holder made of Australian woods – and the other a Smoking Cap – which though you do not smoke may be of some little use to you on board a ship.
With my very best regards,
Believe Me
My Dear Sir William
Yours Most Sincerely
B.I. Macleay'

Nine years older than Macleay, Sir William Macarthur was a member of another highly successful family of early Australian settlers. As well as farming sheep and cattle, he also established some of the first vineyards in Australia and was instrumental in spreading viniculture across the colony. He was an old family friend of the Macleays and did his best to mediate on the quarrel that arose over a substantial financial loan James Macleay had made to his brother George in the late 1850s.

Godstone church is only a few miles away from Bletchingley where Sir George was to create his famous gardens at Pendell Court. But when his wife died in 1869 he had yet to decide where, if at all, he would make a permanent home. The reason he chose Godstone church for his wife's burial and monument – and later his own – was that he was already very familiar with this particular part of Surrey. Until their departure for Australia in 1826, the Macleay family had lived at nearby Tilbuster Lodge. Godstone churchyard has a tomb where four of Sir George's sisters, who died between 1812 and 1820, are buried.

Barbara Macleay's monument is inside the church in the Macleay Chapel. The chapel was created during the church's restoration by Sir George Gilbert Scott in 1872. Scott, one of the best known of all Victorian architects, responsible for building, among many other iconic structures, the Albert Memorial,

St. Pancras Station and the Foreign Office, lived nearby in a house called Rook's Nest. It seems likely Macleay took a close personal interest in the decoration of the chapel as it reflects the family's enduring interest in plants and insects. The remarkable ornamental scheme includes hand painted specimens of the Australian butterfly Macleay's Swallowtail, *Graphium macleayanus,* and the Plume Poppy, *Macleaya cordata.* Both were named to honour George's father, Alexander. Once Sir George decided to settle permanently at Pendell Court he was to use Scott again.

As well as being renowned for the extent of his natural history collections, Alexander Macleay had also been acclaimed for the gardens he created at the new family home he had built in Australia: Elizabeth Bay House in Sydney. Its grounds were notable in the 1830s for the unusual manner in which he combined elements of the native Australian flora with his own extensive and exotic collections of bulbs, orchids and ferns. The fact that such extravagance was drawing him towards bankruptcy, never seemed to bother him.

George managed to avoid becoming entangled in his father's increasingly complex financial affairs.

They were solved, in the end, by the intervention of his eldest son, William Sharp Macleay, who by 1846 had generously taken over all his father's many debts and kept him out of the Insolvency Court. Remarkably, rather than thank him, Alexander Macleay insisted he would never talk to his saviour again. He relented a little in 1847 when his wife Eliza, William's mother died, but they were still barely speaking when Alexander died the following year.

George had managed his financial affairs much more shrewdly. He survived the Australian recession of the 1840s and by the mid-1850s owned over 200,000 acres and was a very rich man. In 1859 he decided to leave Australia for good and live abroad. Using the profits gained through either selling or renting out his extensive Australian properties, George and his wife travelled widely in Britain and Europe, enjoying a lavish lifestyle. In 1869 he was knighted and widowed in the same year.

William Borrer died in 1862. On September 28th 1863, just before Charles took up what was to be only his second job, with William Saunders (1809-1879) – another member of the Linnean Society – Charles and Emily Rowland were married in St. Nicholas's

Church in Brighton. They were breaking the law. Since 1835 it had been illegal for a widower to marry the sister of his deceased wife. This prohibition, based on flimsy biblical precedents and hopeless science, was not lifted until 1907. Those who could afford it – such as the Pre-Raphaelite painter Holman Hunt whose matrimonial circumstances matched Charles Green's almost exactly – simply evaded the problem by marrying overseas. Little or no stigma was attached to such couples on their return to England; although in Holman Hunt's case his fellow Pre-Raphaelite, the sculptor Thomas Woolner never spoke to him again. (Holman Hunt married Edith Waugh, his deceased wife Fanny's sister. Woolner was married to Alice, another of the Waughs).

Charles and Emily could afford neither the time nor the money to travel. Charles was about to start a new, high profile job at William Saunders's house 'Hillfield' in Reigate. If he and Emily remained unmarried but continued to live together they risked possible exposure, and perhaps even dismissal. Their pragmatic solution was to take themselves out of the orbit of the little town of Henfield where everyone knew them - Charles had lived there for over twenty years, Emily more than ten – vanish momentarily into the easy-going anonymity of Brighton where the clergy wouldn't ask too many difficult questions, and then reappear in Surrey as a respectable married couple. They were not unusual in acting this way. A Royal Commission in 1848 revealed that 90% of 1384 illegal marriages studied in a three month period had been between widowers and their deceased wife's sister.

Charles Green was 37 when he married for the second time, Emily was 36. They had no children of their own.

❁   ❁   ❁

By a remarkable chance – it was found in a junk shop in 1990 – a photograph of Green survives from his time with Saunders. Holding a potted fern in his left hand, his penknife in his right, wreathed in the side-whiskers that seem to be *de rigeur* for the contemporary head gardener, the albumen print shows him standing quite composed in front of what may well be the celebrated Hillfield Fernery. He stands very calm and still as the photographer exposes his plate.

The complexity of Green's job as head gardener to William Saunders is breath-taking. These extracts from *The Gardener's Chronicle* of 1872 give an indication not only of the depths of knowledge and practical skills routinely required by head gardeners in the second half of the nineteenth century, but also a context within which to view Green's subsequent work at Pendell Court.

'In this garden, which, among other curiosities, compels Fuchsia to do duty as bedding plants, there are at least 20,000 species of plants grown in the garden, in some form or another. Every nook and corner, every house, every pit, every rockery, every border, teems with interesting plants of some sort or other.'

'Of Orchids, the number grown here is legion, and several houses are assigned to them. Mr. Saunders does not confine his attention to the large flowered showy sections, but includes in his collections a veritable host of the smaller flowering kinds, whose blossoms yield in nothing but size to their larger compeers.'

Charles Green

'Their beauty is, when looked for, quite as striking, often more so; while their conformation is very generally more interesting and extraordinary. Orchid growers, enamoured of the more garish flowers, have sportively denominated the house in

The Orchid House at Hillfield

which these little gems are grown as The Refugium, *a name which the owner has accepted, and made the title of an illustrated work descriptive of these and other treasures. And the Refugium is well filled; the refuge Orchids swarm everywhere; above, below, on each side; and to make room for more, an ingenious device is adopted, vis: that of erecting curved or bowed wire trellises, along the sides of the houses near the glass; on these bows the tiny Orchids cluster. Too thick, we hear someone say; not a bit of* it. The Orchids are in the finest health and vigor; the plants are not large, but they are in perfect health; and the roots they make.'

'If we were to describe literally a Catasetum of no great size, we saw hanging in a basket from the roof, we should scarcely be believed. Equally remarkable is the manner in which the roots in other cases cover the pots with a perfect net-work, creeping from pot to pot; more as "Creeping Jenny" would do, than like an ordinary Orchid. The secret of this unusually luxuriant root growth, Mr. Saunders believes, lies in the due aeration of the roots. He is a great advocate for the free access of air to the roots; and when the peculiar habit of orchids is considered, and the special structure of their roots borne in mind, there can be no doubt as to the soundness of Mr. Saunders' physiology.'

'In another direction is a Cattleya House, elsewhere a cool Orchid House, facing the North, constructed of boarding only, with provision for keeping the frost out and nothing beyond. The air here is still cool and moist, the light tempered, and the plants seem as healthy, firm and green as so many cabbage plants. Nothing could be better for the particular kinds of Orchids, and the particular uses for which it is intended.'

On several occasions throughout the article – there was so much information to impart it was split over two editions of the *Chronicle* – Green and Saunders, servant and master, are given equal status.

'If a stranger plant arrives, the first question put by Mr Saunders and his gardener, Mr Green, is not, 'What is it?' but 'Where does it come from? Under what conditions can we grow it naturally? How can we best make it adapt itself to the conditions we can offer it?' In other words How can we grow it?... Books, plates, magnifying glasses, dissecting needles now come into play; the plant is determined, if it be in a sufficiently developed state for the purpose; if not, it is put at once under such treatment as Mr Saunders and his excellent gardener, Mr Green, are enabled from their great knowledge and experience, to adopt as most fitting under the circumstances.'

'Not far from here is a remarkable collection of ivies, growing over poles...It is to be wished that Mr

Saunders or Mr Green would give us detailed notes on the growths of these several kinds.'

'Saxifrages, Sedums and Sempirvivams are also grown here in great profusion. The mode found most satisfactory by Mr Green...is to grow them is shallow pans sunk a short distance in the ground. These may be moved from place to place as seasons or other exigencies require.'

'The mere labelling so vast a collection is no trifling matter; and when we state, as we can truly, that the whole establishment is in excellent order, we pay no empty or unmeaning compliment to the zeal and skill of the gardener, Mr Green.'

A year later Green's world fell apart. After the dramatic collapse of his maritime insurance interests in 1873 Saunders suddenly found himself facing almost complete financial ruin. In a desperate bid to raise funds he was forced to sell at auction in April 1874 all his treasured collections. These included: stuffed birds, birds' eggs, geological specimens, fossils, porcelain, silver, wine, shells and, of course, his remarkable collection of plants. It is likely that

Green was allowed to keep some of the latter to help him start up the ill-fated nursery business that he ran rather ineffectually until employed by Macleay two years later. As one of his friends wrote after his death:

'Of all the plant growers that I have ever known, Green seemed to me to individualise and love his flowers with an affection I have never seen equalled. As a proof of this I may mention that he gave to me as the reason of relinquishing his nursery at Reigate…that he could not bear to part with the plants he had been tending for years. I remember his saying that to me in quite a broken-hearted sort of way, and as a nurseryman's business consists in passing things rapidly through his hands, Green soon had enough of it, and he was much more happy at Pendell Court. How successfully he managed that most splendid collection not a few can remember, but I have put together these few remarks to emphasise the fact that he loved his flowers as much as most men love their own children.'

It's noteworthy that one of the parents of the *Streptocarpus* hybrid Green created only a year or so after the abrupt dismantling of the garden at Hillfield, was *Streptocarpus saundersii*. Using a plant named after his late master to create something new of his own, was as natural a form of homage as any gardener could pay.

❁   ❁   ❁

The collections sold on the bankruptcy of William Wilson Saunders were typical of those amassed – and in times of hardship, sold – by gentlemen collectors of the 19th century. Sir George's elder brother, William Sharp Macleay, had managed somehow to preserve their father's natural history collections when dealing with his parent's hopeless debts. When William died in 1865 he bequeathed everything his father had compiled, along with his own enormous number of specimens, to his cousin, William John Macleay. He, in his turn, passed everything – supplemented with his own vast collections – to the University of Sydney where this astonishing array of insects, animals, sea creatures, corals, fossils, fish, birds and bone formed the basis of what is now the Macleay Museum.

Unlike his close relations, Sir George had shown little interest in collecting for posterity. His interest was always firmly in the present. Before he purchased Pendell Court Sir George lived for a while in Smyrna where he was sold a number of statues from classical antiquity. He seems to have lent them for a while to what later became the Victoria and Albert Museum and then, in 1881, gave the whole collection to his old friend Sir Charles Nicholson. In 1899 a fire destroyed Sir Charles's house, and the only survivor of the collection was a marble Hermes which is now the Nicholson Museum at the University of Sydney.

Macleay's decision to create a notable garden came when he was well into his sixties. His wife had died in 1869, the year he was knighted, and he had first rented Pendell Court sometime soon afterwards. In July 1870, J.D. Hooker, then Director of Kew, mentioned a visit he had made there in a letter he wrote to Charles Darwin. The census taken in April 1871 gives a neat summary of the style in which Macleay lived. The running of the house was in the hands of his unmarried sister-in-law, Jane. She communicated her wishes to Barbara Gunn, the Scottish housekeeper and Francis Gillham, the butler. Other staff who lived in the big house itself included the Cook, a Footman, Housemaid, Laundry Maid and a Page.

In 1875 George Macleay was made a Knight Commander of the Order of St Michael and St George. Perhaps it was this particular honour that spurred him on to buy, rather than simply continue to rent, Pendell Court. The sale was delayed for some time by a complex legal query that his lawyers took to the Court of Chancery in 1875. But by 1876 the sale was complete. The long wait for the legal ruling turned out be fortuitous as, when the case was finally resolved, Charles Green, whose horticultural, botanical and practical gardening knowledge were to prove crucial in bringing his new master's vision to fruition, was looking for new employment.

Despite Green's recent failure as a nurseryman, there would have been little surprise in horticultural and scientific circles when Macleay chose his first head gardener. He came with the highest recommendations from his previous employer. Saunders shared Macleay's interests and had met with him on many occasions in London. For Saunders was not only a fellow member of the Linnean Society, being elected in 1833, but also its treasurer from 1861 to 1873 during the period when Macleay served on its Council. He was also a vice-president of the Royal Horticultural Society.

Hillfield was proof, should Macleay have needed or wanted it, that the fame of a great garden, and consequently its owner, was no longer confined to its own neighbourhood, county or even country. The picture of the Fernery appeared as the frontispiece to the December 1873 edition of an American gardening publication, *The Horticulturist,* edited by one Henry Williams. With the usual contemporary transatlantic disregard for copyright he had also lifted most of the accompanying text from the *Gardener's Chronicle.*

With Green at the helm, the property secured and Sir George's fortune apparently indestructible, the stage was set for a truly dramatic finale.

❀ ❀ ❀

Three letters written by Charles Green survive. They are dated April 13th 1877, April 8th 1878 and April 20th 1879. Sir George spent these first winters abroad and Green sent regular reports to his master on how his new gardens were progressing. Green writes in the copperplate script he learnt at school – very unlike Sir George's almost illegible scrawl – and expresses himself in rambling, barely punctuated, sometimes slightly contorted prose. As he writes, the cadences of his broad Sussex accent come through clearly.

The letters offer a fascinating insight into how much authority Macleay had delegated to Green, how confidently he moved in the elite levels of horticultural society, how at ease he was with plants, how he was still slightly uneasy in his relationship with his master, and how the gardens at Pendell Court had already become the heart of an international plant collecting operation.

The first letter, April 13th 1877, is headed *'Reigate',* implying that Charles and Emily had yet to move into their house on the Pendell Court estate.

'Sir Geo.

I fear you have expected to hear from me before this, the delay I trust you will excuse. I was anxious to collect what matter I could on various subjects to communicate at one, in the first instance I thought you would be glad to know about the plants sent off from Portugal, these arrive safe yesterday bulbs in good order, cuttings doubtful. I also have learned from Mr Smith at Kew that a case of plants are expected from Sydney a portion of its contents are for Sir Geo., on arrival Mr S. will let me know and I will go & attend to them I judge the case to be the one mention by Sir W. Macarthur, when I go to Kew I will see after more herbaceous pts. etc. I have not as yet been able to get them…'

Sir William Macarthur, the old family friend, also loved gardening. He had introduced the camellia to Australia, and had one of the first glasshouses on the continent in which he cultivated orchids.

'I was truly sorry to learn again from your letter the sad condition of the Orchids again sent to Sydney, one almost despairs of success after such failures however I will do my best again. I have not yet purchased any more Orchids but will when another opportunity offers; I have just been to the Bot. Gardens, Oxford and met with a good collection of aquatic and other plants liberally offered by Mr Baxter the curator I brought away some ten or twelve Nuphari x Nymphae also a good strong plant of Papyrus antiquora which could not get at Kew as their plant was weak.'

The Baxter whom Charles Green met was William Hart Baxter, the son of William Baxter, who had been previously held the post of curator, or head gardener, of the Botanic Gardens at Oxford. It was during the first William Baxter's tenure, in 1851, that the Tropical Lily House was built. This was where the *Nymphae* were grown. Bizarrely its distinctive glass domed roof appears in the background to the illustration Tenniel drew in 1865 for Lewis Carroll's *Alice in Wonderland* where the Queen is shouting *'Off with her head!'*

'Dr Hooker' was the famous botanist and explorer, Joseph Dalton Hooker (1817-1911) who had succeeded his father as Director of Kew Gardens in 1865. Hooker was another Victorian scientist who fell foul of Richard Owen's petty jealousies. It took a special Parliamentary inquiry to uncover the malicious damage Owen had attempted to do to Hooker's reputation. Hooker had his revenge however as, in 1873, much to Owen's disgust, he was elected President of the Royal Society, the oldest and most revered Scientific Society in Britain.

'Fortune's yellow Rose' is a reference to an ancient tea rose named after its collector, Robert Fortune, who discovered it in a Chinese garden in 1845.

'Dr Hooker and Mr Smith I have seen and I shall probably get many good plants by the time you return. I cannot as yet meet with Fortune's yellow rose. I am getting on with the Houses and hope to have them in order before you return several good things have flowered, such as Masdevallia davisi ... Cattleya citrina ... large Crinum ... Tillandsia ... very pretty sp. Several others, the Bromelias are doing well planted in moss on the wall. The tree ferns are breaking well and some Telopea's are growing.'

Masdevallia davisi, was a beautiful yellow orchid that had only recently been discovered in 1873 by Walter Davis while on a plant hunting expedition to Peru sponsored by the famous London firm of nurserymen, James Veitch and Sons. *Cattleya citrina* was an orchid from Mexico. Exactly which species of *Crinum* Green was describing is unclear, but like the rest of its family it would have had large, showy, flowers. *Tillandsia* are epiphytes, plants that grow without soil, and are usually found growing on other, larger plants. They are related to the *Bromelias.* The *Telopeas* would have also been known to Macleay as *Watarahs* – one of the most spectacular garden plants found in New South Wales.

'The outdoor Garden such as new planted shrubs etc. all seem to look well, I have not as yet been able to finish planting the new Rock work but hope to in a few days. I could not meet with Mr Carruthers until Wednesday last, I learn from him that he has found the oak timber for panelling, but is rather doubtful if it will quite answer the purpose & he tells me the work is progressing favourably towards being finished by the end of May,

I am Sir Geo

your Obedient Servant

C Green

P.S. Major Macleay has written to Mrs Green about 2 cows which are sent over.'

Major Macleay seems to have been a distant Scottish cousin of Sir George's, but exactly where the cows had been sent from remains unclear.

Green's second letter is dated April 8th 1878. It is headed *'Pendell Court'*.

'Sir Geo.

I trust you will not think that I am falling short of my duty by not writing before this, I have been waiting these last few days expecting a package of

Orchids from the Neilgherry hills, dispatched by Capt. F. Onslow, as I learn from Miss Onslow of Send Grove, but they have not as yet turned up...'

Francis Onslow was a professional soldier serving in India. The Neilgherry Hills are located in Southern India, roughly between what was known then as Bangalore and Madurai. A few months later, in November 1878, Francis saw action in the far north of the country at the start of the Second Afghan War. He was the nephew of Sir George as his mother, George's sister Rosa Roberta, had married Arthur Onslow who, by the 1870s, had made his home at Send Grove House near Woking in Surrey. To add yet another strand to the complex relationships that existed between early Australian colonial families, Francis's brother Arthur married into the Macarthur family; his wife later changing her name to Macarthur-Onslow.

'...you will I think be pleased to hear that a box of terrestrial Orchids have reached here from Rome in capital condition packed in moss I believe every tuber will grow, and some will probably flower enough to tell something what they are, in sorting up,

to the best of my judgement there seems something like twelve or fifteen different kinds, six separate ones were labelled viz. Epipactis eusifolia, Serapias, Orchis simia, O. militaris, O. pisca O. hircina, about 200 tubers in all.'

Changes in the classification of plants over the last 150 years, coupled with the fact that Green's writing of botanic names can occasionally be difficult to interpret, means sometimes it can be unclear as to exactly which species of orchid he is describing. *Orchis militaris,* the soldier orchid, and *Orchis hircina*, as the lizard orchid was known then, can both be found in Northern Europe. The mirror orchid, *Orchis speculum,* and the *Serapias* are generally found further south towards the Mediterranean. *Trichopilia suavis* originated in Central America. The presence of all these, alongside *Maxillaria venusta* from Columbia, *Nanodes Medusae* from Equador and *Angraecum sesquipidale* from Madagascar, underlines the breadth and diversity of the collection that Macleay and Green were building up at Pendell Court.

'I think you would also like to know that the Orchids from Seville last season are now flowering & very good they are, Ophrys speculum and one or two I do not know, the indoor Orchids are coming on, tho' we have as yet very cold weather mixed with frost and snow. ... the large Crinums are flowering in the tank, one had 26 flowers this was much admired at S. Kensington on the 2nd inst. People seem to know but little about these fine things.'

South Kensington was the home of the Royal Horticultural Society from 1861 until 1888.

'I am glad to say that I have found someone to do the grafting which I got finished on Saturday, and hope satisfactory, the leakage at the bay has been stopped, and shall probably have the Trout in this week. I am getting on with the new water tank and Mr Waycott is preparing for the Fernhouse, plants and flowers outdoors, on account of cold weather do not look so happy as when you left, there was a sale of Orchids on Thursday last on which I ventured 2 guineas for a good healthy plant of Angraecum sesquipidale ... & 30/- for an imported plant of Nanodes Medusa with six or seven growths.'

The *'bay'* that Green mentions is the earth bank that served to dam the lake. Thomas Speed was the Head Gardener at Chatsworth, the celebrated gardens of the Duke of Devonshire.

'Plants ordered from Ware are sent and planted, also a hamper from Kew, containing a portion of the plants I selected when there. Mr. Speed of Chatsworth has invited me to the Gardens, and with your permission I note a few things for exchange (illegible) an opportunity for a day there when I get the houses a little more in order, allow me to say, I hope all have fair weather, health, and enjoyment & that I shall soon hear of the dispatch of some interesting plants for Pendell

I am your obedient Servant

Chas Green.'

The '*plants ordered from Ware*' were most likely ones bought from Thomas Ware's Hale Farm Nursey in Tottenham.

The third letter is dated April 20th 1879. It is headed *'Pendell Court'*. Quoting it uninterrupted allows a fuller picture of how Green's interests, duties, priorities and concerns spilled out onto the page as he wrote. The orchids he prefixes with the letter *'D'* are all of the genus *'Dendrobium'*. In 1882, Miss Ellen Taylor published her delightful book: *'Madeira, Its Scenery, and How to See It, With Letters of a Year's Residence, and Lists of the Trees, Flowers, Ferns and Seaweeds.'*

'Sir Geo.

I have just unpacked a large case of Ferns etc from Miss Taylor Madeira, about 150 plants, for the most part in fair condition and I think will grow. I intend to keep them together for a week or two before being planted in the fernery that I might watch them a little closer. I will also this week get the plants & cuttings ready to send to Miss Taylor such as I mentioned in my last letter, we are still getting the weather very cold so that things in general have not advanced much tho' I am glad to say we do not get much frost, but on Easter day a heavy fall of snow.
I cannot send as good a supply of flowers to the Ladies as I could wish, however, I send all I possibly can, the peaches and nectarines in fruit house have set well and swelling off, so that if all goes well there will be a fine crop. Amaryllis are flowering well and

a few Orchids have been good such as D. suavissimum, this I took to S. Kensington, D. pulchellum now in flower, D. Devonianum C. Loddigesii ... Dipodium coming on nicely in flower. Echium...a picture with eight spikes of beautiful azure blue flowers this I hope to show at S. Kensington on the 22nd, Mackaya bella I have already shown and was much admired, and but little known; what a grand plant when seen as now with over 400 flowers, a woodcut is being prepared for Grd. Chron. Bignonia speciosa is now flowering in new house. Alpinia nutans just showing fl. I have planted on back wall all the Cacti we have and hope to get some more from Kew before you return, Fuchsia arborea is flowering, Aster agophyllus ... the Telopea plants are doing well but I fear no flowers this season. Hardy flowers as yet are few, Primula stuartii is very pretty with its bright rose colored flowers, many of our outdoor shrubs begin to show the effects of the long winter, the leaves of the Common Laurels and Portugal's look very rusty, yet with a little cutting will come to rights some plants of Cistus have escaped, Chamaerops not hurt, Camellias and host of the other planted by the lily pond are alive. I rather doubt about Rubus *eglanteria. Lilium giganteum is coming up strong & bids fair to flower. I have received from Mrs Gunn your note of April 1st and am sorry that my two previous letters had not then reached you. I fear you will think I have not written so often as you wished it is in consequence of the continuing cold weather that I felt there was so little fresh in the gardens to report on. I mentioned before that Russell is gone, but his goods are still in the house, am I right to ask what about the garden there? I hope not to ask a wrong question.*

I am your Obedient Servant
Charles Green'

❀ ❀ ❀

At its peak in the mid-1880s, Pendell Court was essentially two gardens. What was most important to both Macleay and Green was the extensive plant collection that was grown under glass. It was almost the private equivalent of a university, or national, Botanic Garden containing numerous examples, from all around the world, of unusual and exotic plants. Some were so rare they were sent to Kew to be studied, or used as the source for authoritative illustrations in the *Botanical Magazine.* In many ways its specialised nature reflected the insect collections built up by Macleay's father, brother and cousin that were so extensive they furnished many of the 'type specimens' that enabled entomologists to identify securely individual species.

The outdoor gardens, although of less importance to Macleay and Green, are of particular interest as they put into practice the theories of William Robinson, the most effective horticultural revolutionary of his time. Once again the Linnean Society provided the essential link. Robinson was elected in 1866 when both Macleay and Saunders were members of its governing body. It comes as no surprise to learn that both men were keen to further Robinson's views.

Robinson's great desire was to revolutionise Victorian gardening by sweeping away what he saw as the restrictive formality of geometrically precise flowerbeds, typically filled with thousands of bedding plants, in favour of a much freer style of informal planting that relied far more on a range of hardy perennials. Robinson had founded his weekly, illustrated, magazine *The Garden* in 1871 to propagandise his theories. He also bombarded the gardening world with a stream of books. His hugely influential *The Wild Garden* first appeared in 1870 and its content was evidently taken to heart by Saunders who, by 1872, allowed no bedding plants in his garden at all. Robinson's description of Pendell Court in the *English Flower Garden* of 1883, shows how closely Green had continued to follow the key tenets of this new style of outdoor gardening.

'It is a great pleasure to see a beautiful old house, made to live in, with nothing to keep one away from the door but the pleasant Grass. From a gardening standpoint there are three distinct views of it which are good; first that of the lawn in front of the house, which, when we saw it, was a flowery meadow yet uncut, and no bed or other impediments between the point of view and the house, with a group of some fine trees on either hand. It was a poem in building and lawn. Quite on the other side a border of flowers and a wall of climbers ran from the house. ...

'Another view of the house from across the water, showing its west end is also very beautiful. There is a wild Rose bush on the right and a tuft of Flag leaves on the left; before the beholder, the water and its Lilies; then a smooth, gently rising lawn creeping up to the windows, which on this side are all wreathed

with lovely white climbing Roses. It will be observed that all these different views of the same house, although quite distinct, are all marked by the absence of the impediments of which a false art frequently places near our houses – that is to say, formal patterns in beds, fountains and statues, and other like objects which destroy the repose so desirable in such places.'

The plants used in and around the edges of the lawns at Pendell Court to aid the creation of such fashionable simplicity were not necessarily native to either the county or the country. Robinson, unlike his contemporary the Arts and Crafts designer and writer William Morris, who railed in 1882 against the introduction of foreign plants in English gardens, was keen to use anything that suited. Whereas Morris might fulminate about:

'...plants which are curiosities only, which nature meant to be grotesque, not beautiful, and which are generally the growth of hot countries where things sprout over - quick and rank. Take note that the strangest of these come from the jungle and the tropical waste, from places where man is not at

home...'

Robinson was much more catholic in his approach.

'This term [The Wild Garden] is especially applied to the placing of perfectly hardy exotic plants in places, and under conditions, where they will become established and take care of themselves...the Winter Aconite flowering under a grove of naked trees in February...the Snowflake growing abundantly in meadows by the Thames side; by the perennial Lupine dyeing an islet with its purple in a Scotch river; and by the Apennine Anemone staining an English wood before the blooming our Bluebells.'

❈ ❈ ❈

Much of the astonishing transformation that Charles Green masterminded at Pendell Court took less than five years to complete. In 1881 he was able to show off much of what had been achieved in so short a time to one of *The Garden's* most trusted writers, Frederick Harvey, who later became the magazine's editor. Much of what Harvey recorded on that first visit formed the basis for the text that accompanied the illustration of Pendell Court in

William Robinson's *The English Flower Garden.* As founder and editor of *The Garden,* Robinson presumably regarded his staff's work as his own.

Harvey took care when confirming with Green the details of his visit to be very clear at which of the two stations that served Pendell Court he was intending to alight. Both the South Eastern Railway and the London and Brighton Railway shared the line that headed south from the terminus at London Bridge, but years of rivalry between the two companies meant that although both used Redhill Junction, only SER trains stopped at Merstham. Buying the wrong ticket or getting on the wrong train would mean there would be nobody waiting at the station to drive Mr Harvey the two or three miles to the house.

Had Mr Harvey travelled by the South East Railway, and stepped off the train at Merstham, he would have approached the house and grounds from the north-west. That route would have meant his first view of Sir George's most recent improvements was the lodge cottage newly built at one end of his new, curved, carriage drive. Although North Lodge was used by head gardeners in the 20th century, Charles and Emily remained in the quarters they had first been allocated, in a cluster of buildings about a quarter of a mile to the south-west of the Court itself. Another part of this complex was occupied by the coachman and his wife. Macleay's priorities were clear – any new domestic building works for domestic staff would be delayed until the new gardens were complete. He did, however, commission a new billiard room from Sir Gilbert Scott. The architect's fees were £142, the building costs, £2000. It was completed in 1878, the year of Scott's death.

The Lake at Pendell Court

The orchard at the bottom of the Greens' garden disappeared soon after they moved in to allow the old lake to be widened and to be given what was thought to be a more decorative outline. Both the scale and the speed of the remodelling were remarkable. As early as 1878, *The Gardener's Chronicle* was describing the lake as being:

'...a piece of water, so artfully managed by the designer that it is difficult to realise that this pretty natural looking lakelet, with its flower decked islets, was only a very few years ago a straight ditch'.

Frederick Harvey chose to alight at Redhill Junction which gave him a far more dramatic initial view of his eventual destination. Following what is now the A25 out of Redhill, travelling on through Nutfield, and then turning sharp left by the Red Lion, he discovered Pendell Court at the bottom of a winding lane:

'...a grand old house embowered in perpetual greenery, rising direct from the pleasant lawn, which slopes down to the edge of a small, but cleverly formed lake.'

Sir George Macleay

Macleay's new drive was designed to bring visitors to the front door of the old Jacobean house via some very modern planting.

'Near the base of some of the trees along the drive one may notice that the turf is not mown, but, on the contrary, the red wood Lychnis and Foxgloves, and the large Grasses and other wild plants are allowed to have their own way. These, however, mark the place where many Crocuses,

Meadow Saffrons, Daffodils, Violets, Polyanthuses and Snowdrops are at rest. In spring and autumn they jewel the ground around these trees – another arrangement enabling one to have bits of "wild garden" in the pleasure garden.'

Having been greeted at the front door, Mr Harvey was conducted through the ground floor drawing rooms with their elegant 18th century painted and plastered ceilings, to the south side of the house and handed over to Charles Green via the garden door. The broad gravel path they stepped out onto offered them the opportunity to visit either the grounds or the glasshouses. Saving the best till last, they took the former option first.

A junction in the path led them diagonally across the lawn towards a footbridge at the end of the lake. They paused to view the:

'...grand specimens of the two Gunneras both of which delight in the moisture obtained from the water-logged subsoil."

In the first section of his book, *The English Flower Garden,* Robinson includes and praises a plan of a garden designed by Robert Marnock. It bears many similarities to the remodelling supervised by Green at Pendell Court. In the plan, just as at Pendell Court, a sloping lawn, with no flowerbeds, only carefully placed clumps of trees, runs down to the edge of a lake. Starting from the side, not the front, of the house *"one bold walk"* leads the visitor on a winding, circular tour that takes in both the best possible views and the best examples of the gardener's craft.

It is still just possible today at Pendell Court to identify a sunken garden, to trace the original positions of some old yew hedges, now grown into tall trees, circumnavigate the overgrown edges and bed of a second, now completely dried-up, lake with its partially buried brick dam and the remnants of its attendant water features, and stroll through a jungle of hugely overgrown evergreens interspersed with a few surviving specimen trees of the pleasure gardens. The sunken garden was one of the few earlier features of Pendell Court that survived Macleay's remodelling. It seems, for some reason, to have been allowed to preserve its more traditional forms of planting.

'...a sunk garden of oblong form and geometric design, the beds filled in with bedding plants of the usual type; this sunk border with its sloping banks and geometric parterres is in strict harmony with the architectural character of the mansion...'

In the 1860s what Macleay and Green turned into the pleasure garden – an area some little distance from the house and intended for gentle strolls through a softly undulating landscape – was open farmland, dotted with only a few trees. A public footpath ran alongside this area, just as it does today. Macleay felt no need to build a wall around his estate, but a belt of Cherry and Portugal Laurels, Yew and Holly was planted to create a solid evergreen border between this public right of way and Macleay's private land. His paths wound their way under the shade of some of the more common conifers available: the Himalayan Cedar, the Incense Cedar, the Austrian Pine and the Lawson Cypress. Their presence, or more accurately the absence of any more unusual specimen trees either here or elsewhere in the grounds, underlines the fact that Macleay and Green's real priorities lay within the glasshouses.

Despite Green and Macleay's enjoyment of the exotic and 'showy', Robinson's ideas concerning harmony, taste and the laws of Nature were also important to them, and their efforts to match their planting with the natural setting of the house, were highly praised.

'Nature has done much for this garden and its surroundings. Soft undulations, wood-capped, and with green valleys, letting in more distant views, form as it were the setting for the garden itself...'

'...a garden that one cannot help admiring for its simple beauty and for the wealth of varied plant life which it contains. Here one finds no costly terraces, but a grand old house, embowered in perpetual greenery, rising direct from the pleasant lawn...No intricate parterre cuts the turf into plots; on the contrary there are only a few beds of the simplest possible forms...and these and with a few fine old trees are the only interruptions to the continuous roll of lawn from the walls of the house to the boundaries of the garden on nearly all sides.'

Comfortable in the knowledge that the outdoor, and most accessible, areas of the gardens at Pendell Court fitted his magazine's, and therefore his master's, philosophy of gardening, Harvey accompanied Green to the heart of Pendell Court – the glasshouses.

The area covered by Macleay's own glasshouses at Pendell Court quickly grew to be greater than the footprint of his mansion. Most of the hot houses were purpose built, although a Mushroom house that was already on site was converted and the rubble and galleted wall that had enclosed the original 17th century gardens was also incorporated into the design. One side of this wall, the most northerly stretch that ran east to west, was used as the back wall of a bothy; the other side, south-facing, was used as the back wall to a range of glasshouses that stretched for almost fifty metres. The bothy was built as a dormitory for garden boys and single journeymen. It shared the main chimney stack for the Tropical House so the more lowly members of the resident garden staff were conveniently housed to enable the boiler fires to be kept burning throughout the night

The Tropical House was huge, the size of a modern two-storey, three bedroom, town house. But even so it was deemed inadequate for the profusion and variety of plants Macleay wished to be seen to be displayed, and so the rag-tag collection of sheds, farmyard walls and buildings that lay to the north of the old kitchen garden were swept away and replaced with a new coach house, stables and an area of glass that covered over a thousand square metres.

Green guided Harvey through almost the twenty different houses. They began by passing through a Vinery; the variety of grape growing there, *Gros Clamar*, was capable of yielding fruit as late as October. The same house contained an equally productive specimen of a Guava. This neat introduction to Green's ability to grow difficult and unusual plants was amplified by the contents of the next stop on the tour, the Tropical House itself.

The Tropical House was the largest and the tallest of all Macleay's hothouses. One of Charles Green's trademarks at Pendell Court was to try and conceal the presence of hot-water pipes and other harsh structural lines with little pieces of rock amongst which he planted ferns and other *'fine-foliaged plants'*, but The Tropical House had no staging to hide as Green preferred to plant out, wherever possible, in 'free soil.' His method seemed to be working well as *The Garden's* correspondent wrote most appreciatively of the flourishing condition of the Blood Bananas from Sumatra, the Forest Bell Bush from South Africa, and the Crape Myrtle from the Far East. These were just a few of the host of exotic plants that Green would point out to his master's visitors as they followed the winding path – another innovation in the usually more formal layout of glasshouses - edged with variegated grasses, club mosses and ferns, that led from one end of The Tropical House to the other.

Leaving behind the Night Flowering Cactus planted beneath the Rex Begonia, artfully arranged to wind its way through the dead branches of an old pear tree, the Bird's Head Birthwort, climbing up to the roof and after finding time to scribble down at Green's dictation the *Tibouchina elegans* tastefully intertwined with a *Stigmaphyllum ciliatum,* Harvey found no respite from exotics as he entered the next, smaller house. Here he encountered *'a collection of various plants of small size'* offset by a dramatically large specimen of *Medinilla magnifica* – commonly known now as the Philippine orchid – that was almost three metres across. Glancing up at the roof he noted *'...climbers of various kinds, Aristolochias and Passifloras being specially fine...'* There were hanging baskets, too, that held different varieties of *Aeschynanthus*, a genus of epiphytes from Southeast Asia.

A smaller house, with a much lower roof, holding beds of *'reputedly difficult to manage kinds of bulbs'* led to the next major showpiece, The Fernery. Green had transformed the newly built structure

'...with everywhere a rocky and mossy surface, with the tall dark stems of Tree Ferns for the pillars of the little landscape, so to say, and their graceful crests for its roof.'

The picturesque appearance he was aiming for was that of a fern-filled ravine or gully. The light coming through the roof was muted by carefully deployed plantings of moss, while the beauty of the different ferns that filled every possible nook, ledge and cranny was emphasised by their reflections shimmering in the little pools of water that had been constructed, apparently at random, across the floor. There was also a set of stone steps leading up to a miniature cave and a rustic archway. Another feature of Macleay's Fernery was that plants requiring differing atmospheres and climatic conditions were all grown in the same house. The varying degrees of temperature and humidity were provided mainly by the careful positioning of the ferns in relation to the key sources of light, heat and water.

A temperate, corridor glasshouse with a long border planted out with Bomerea and Fuschias led the visitor to yet another series of specialist collections. First an Orchid House, and then a large tank for aquatics. Yet again Macleay and Green impressed with the breadth and the novelty of their specimens. *Eichhornia azurea,* a rooted water hyacinth from Central and South America, had only just started to be grown in Britain and it made a suitably rare companion for the *Thalia dealbata* that had originated in Mexico, although both must have been dwarfed by the Australian water-lily *Nymphaea gigantean* and the Indian lotus *Nelumbium speciosum.* The margins of the water tank were planted with *Alocasias, Hedychiums* and Egyptian papyrus, while overhead Pitcher plants lurked in hanging baskets.

After even more orchids, and the

'...beautiful little hothouse in which those strange tropical plants, the Bromelias and Tillandsias, are planted out on mossy stems and rocky surfaces, in which they look at home and thrive as well as in their native tropical jungles...'

Harvey and Green emerged into the more familiar territory of the Peach and Fig houses. Beyond them were the pits and cold frames in which Green grew the hardy plants he used to fill in any gaps that might appear in his herbaceous borders. After shaking hands with his knowledgeable host, Mr Harvey, with a full notebook, made his thoughtful way back to London.

One part of his tour would have emphasised to Harvey that what he had seen was still a work in progress and by no means the finished article. The newness of the gardens Green and Macleay were creating together was underlined by the fact that the water tower that was built especially to supply the complex range of glasshouses at Pendell Court was only finally completed in 1881, the year of Harvey's visit. This water tower became the subject of a court case in January 1882 between Sir George and its builder, the latter requesting on completion a sum far greater than his original estimate. After a good deal of wrangling by their legal representatives a price was agreed between both parties. The water tower, incidentally, still stands today, although nothing remains of the huge glasshouses that it once served survive.

❀   ❀   ❀

The picture of the Orchid House at Hillfield gives some indication of how crowded the interiors of the hot houses at Pendell Court may have been, but they are of little help when it comes to imagining just how dramatic an assault on the senses so much tropical colour and perfume must have made. An expectation of all head gardeners was that they should demonstrate their master's munificence and expertise in botany and horticulture not only to the casual visitor, but also to their more learned peers. One accepted way of doing this was by regularly sending examples of their best plants to be viewed at the meetings of the RHS.

'Mr C. Green, gardener to Sir George Macleay, Pendell Court, Bletchingley, sent flowers of Canna iridiflora, var. Ehemanni, of great size and deep crimson colour. A note appended stated that the

plant from which the flowers had been gathered had been in bloom for the past seven months, treated as a sub-aquatic - namely, planted with the crown about 9 inches above the surface of the water in a warm tank devoted to Nymphaeas.'

On the same occasion, but for the benefit of the Fruit rather than the Floral Committee, Green sent a flowering bough of a coffee plant. It was reported in 1881 that Sir George was able to have his breakfast coffee made from the beans that Green was producing in his glasshouses. The fame of the gardens, and their head gardener, spread across the Empire. In June 1882 the *South Australian Weekly Chronicle* informed its readers:

'That gorgeous native of eastern Australia, the Waratah, has recently been grown with wonderful success in England. The Garden, in speaking of this effort of Mr Green (Sir George Macleay's skilful gardener at Pendell Court), says: The latest achievement of Mr Green is the flowering of this gorgeous Australian shrub....The glowing descriptions that travellers have given of it as seen in its native habitats in the "bush" are fully borne

out by the plant now in flower at Pendell Court in one of the large cool greenhouses. It is some 8 or 9 feet high. On the whole it is a most remarkable plant and extremely showy, and the interest attached to it is increased by the fact that it has as yet flowered but once or twice in this country.'

Earlier in 1882, in March, Augusta Sams, who was to marry Sir George eight years later in 1890, had written a lively, rather playful, letter to Edward Knox, the highly successful Australian businessman, banker and devout churchman, who looked after her financial affairs. Augusta is an intriguing figure in the story of Pendell Court. Her exact status in the Macleay household at this time is hard to define. In her letter sent from the Italian villa Sir George had taken by Lake Maggiore in Italy she writes as though she has been an intimate friend of Sir George for some time.

'How very sad the death of Capt. (illegible) is. We heard it here by telegram, it was a great blow to both Sir George and (illegible). We shall probably be here until the middle of June as Sir George is quite turned out of Pendell for the present. Extensive alterations

are going on there which will scarcely be finished before June.'

She signs off:

'My... love to Mrs Knox...with kind regards to yourself in which Sir George joins me. Believe me dear Mr Knox sincerely yours Augusta Sams.'

❁   ❁   ❁

On the 9th of January 1884 Sir Richard Owen wrote to William Robinson to congratulate him on the quality of the engravings that had been used to illustrate *'The English Flower Garden.'* Owen also mentioned that he had written to his friend Sir George to tell him how particularly beautiful was the picture of Pendell Court.

In November of the previous year a near neighbour, Clara Walbey, was moved to express her thoughts about the gardens through what the *Surrey Mirror* gallantly described as 'Poetry':

*'Thou hast an air of olden times,
Thy massive breadth and beauty render,
While ruby leaves from Western Climes.
Deck stately age with New World splendour.'*

Despite her somewhat mannered tone, Clara Walbey managed to identify rather succinctly what was at the heart of Macleay and Green's vision for the Pendell Court: a subtle combination of rare and exotic plants from across the world within a very English setting. The gardens' inclusion in Robinson's book was confirmation of just how successful they had been in realising this dream.

The first January edition of the *Gardeners Chronicle* for 1884 listed the members of the Royal Horticultural Society's Committees for that year. Once again Charles Green's name appeared on the list for the Floral Committee. In the next column was the obituary of Thomas Speed, the Head Gardener at Chatsworth with whom Green had exchanged plants. He had taken his own life.

'Mr Speed suffered greatly from gout, and had been in the habit of taking a medicine which had the effect of causing depression, and the jury returned a verdict of "Suicide during temporary insanity." ...the loss of one of the most helpful of wives, that he had to sustain a few years ago, preyed heavily on his mind, he being helpless at times through the gout, and left with six children to care for. Poor fellow!'

It was widely known, though not reported, that Speed had shot himself. Life continued as normal at Pendell Court. In February one of the journeymen, Mr. W. B. Russell, was looking for a new job and put Green, with whom he had been for six years, down as his referee. At the start of April he was once again amazing the Floral Committee with yet another batch of astonishing plants he had grown.

'The Pendell Court plant is no less than 12 feet high and 6 feet through, truly a marvellous specimen.'

As Green went about his daily duties, so Sir George studiously followed those expected of a Knight Commander of the Order of St. Michael and St. George, and those of a local Lord of the Manor. The latter included being on the Committee of the Bletchingley and Nutfield Cottage Garden Society, although it seems he may have had to miss the annual show as, in the last week of July 1884, he had to be in London to attend a Court levee.

Charles Green also travelled to the capital that month to attend a further meeting of the RHS Floral Committee. July 1884 is the last occasion on which any reference to Charles Green can be found in the gardening press. There is no mention of him again until his obituary appears in December 1886.

What happened to Green is a mystery.

On August 11th 1884 Gerald Waller, a professional plant collector, used the headed notepaper at Pendell Court, where he was staying, to write to Sir William Thistleton-Dyer, the new Director-elect of Kew. His latest collecting trip to Japan had been a fruitful one, in every sense of the word, and he had a variety of seeds, plants – and woodcuts of plants – that he thought would be of interest. He had already given seeds of some unusual Japanese Ipomeas to Sir George and they were doing well under glass. Sir George had also purchased numerous plants of Japanese lotus. There was nothing in Waller's letter to hint that anything might be amiss in Macleay's corner of Paradise.

It was also officially announced in August 1884 that in the following year, 1885, Sir George would represent the colony of New South Wales at the international Postal Congress Union in Lisbon.

That something momentous happened at Pendell Court, at some point, in the latter half of 1884 is clear from Sir George's dramatic decision in December to put up for auction his three beautiful carriage horses, a landau, a brougham, a park phaeton and a tax cart.

Exactly why he did so is another puzzle, on a level with Charles Green suddenly disappearing from his role as Head Gardener. The reason given by the auctioneer for the sale was that Sir George was '...*going abroad and therefore has no further use of them.*' Similarly Macleay's reason given for resigning from the Council of the Surrey Archaeological Society was because he was: '...*leaving England.*' By February of 1885 he had also resigned from the Council of the Royal Colonial Institute. He had been a member since its foundation in 1868.

Sir George's apparently impetuous decision to abandon all that he and Green had created and concentrate, instead, on a new life abroad, coincides exactly with the end of his gardener's glittering career.

It is tempting, in the light of what happened almost ten years later between Augusta and Catherine Aberdeen, to speculate wildly that Miss Sams must have been the cause of Green's departure – a quarrel with him, perhaps, that led to his departure; or a row with Sir George in which she insisted he must choose between the gardens and her? But Augusta's position in 1884, whatever it was, was still insecure. It seems unlikely she would jeopardise the possibility of an eventual marriage and a secure old age.

It is equally unlikely that any sudden decision on Sir George's part to live abroad would cause Green to resign, or turn to drink. Managing the gardens during Macleay's long absences abroad had been part of his job from the beginning, and even if his master was no longer able or prepared to make the gardens his priority it is improbable that Green, a genuinely passionate gardener in charge of a garden that suited his interests exactly, would be unable to adapt to this slightly different situation.

What seems most likely is that Green was suddenly no longer able to carry out his duties because, like poor Thomas Speed at Chatsworth, ill-health prevented him. Perhaps the only way he could bear the pain he suffered was through alcohol. Perhaps his despair at not being able to do the thing he had loved all his working life, made him seek solace and escape at the bottom of a bottle. Perhaps he had been an alcoholic for years and it was only now, in 1884, that his addiction began to interfere with his work.

It may also have been this sudden loss of his trusted gardener that prompted Sir George's impetuous decision to leave and live abroad; perhaps Augusta Sams encouraged him. In the last week of October 1884, she and Sir George went to the funeral of Sir Valentine Fleming who had lived at a house called Holbrook only a few miles away from Pendell Court. When he was a young man, Valentine Fleming had been another who had headed to Australia to try and make his fortune and, once there, he had worked closely in his early years with William Gardner Sams, Augusta's father. Her lively presence at the funeral of his exact contemporary, Sir Valentine was 75 when he died, may have made Sir George think hard about how best to spend his remaining years.

It is also likely that the loss of Green upset him. Green was fifteen years younger than Macleay and had a timeless, ineffable, quality about him. Unlike most gardeners he had never resigned a post or looked to change his employment. Change had always been forced upon him: first by Borrer's death and then by Saunders' bankruptcy. The measured pace of his sheltered working life had enabled him to develop a deep, intuitive, understanding of plants and gardens that owed everything to the total absorption of a true craftsman, and little to the bustling, edgy, outside world of the late Victorian empire. Macleay may have valued and envied his obedient servant in equal measure.

Whatever it was that caused Green to give up his profession at the height of his career, it seems Macleay did his best to stand by him. If the Electoral Rolls are to be believed, Green and his wife Emily continued to have the use of their house on the Pendell Court estate. They appear to have moved to Reigate only shortly before Charles's death on November 11th 1886.

Green's obituary in *The Garden* read:

'...Few men of the present day possessed such an extensive knowledge of plants as Charles Green, and his love for all kinds of plants, especially those out of the ordinary run, was only equalled by his skill in growing them. For upwards of thirty years Mr. Green has been known in connection with garden botany...Unassuming in his manner, ever ready to impart information about plants, he won respect

from everyone. His death is a real loss to horticulture, for it may truly be said that he was the means of preserving many a plant that would have been cast aside in accordance with the vagaries of fashion, and of rescuing other fine plants from the oblivion to which they had fallen...'

On his death certificate the doctor who had treated him made a terse note. Next to where, as cause of death, he recorded *'Acute Alcoholism'*, he also wrote: *'5 days'*. Had Charles's final bout lasted one day less he would have died on the 30th anniversary of his wedding to Lucy.

Green didn't die penniless. He left Emily just over £431 in his will – the equivalent today, perhaps, of £40,000. It was more than his second employer, William Wilson Saunders had been able to bequeath to his widow.

Another member of the gardening staff at Pendell Court died in 1886. The details of the inquest into the death of Christopher Cucksey, aged 76, are a reminder that most gardeners in the 19th century lived a life of hard toil with little recognition and little prospect of a secure or comfortable retirement.

'Christopher Cucksey... met his death by falling downstairs on Saturday last...He was a gardener to Sir George Macleay. About six weeks since the deceased had sprained his foot, which kept him in the house. On Saturday last he went into the village to get shaved, and he returned soon after five o'clock. About nine p.m....witness...heard a fall...she found the deceased at the bottom of the stairs in a sitting position...She sent for a doctor at once, and he came soon after, but the deceased was quite dead....He was not the worse for drink and seemed very well...The Jury returned a Verdict of Accidental Death.'

❁   ❁   ❁

The puzzle as to exactly what had made Sir George suddenly declare his intention of moving abroad deepens when it becomes clear that the sale of his carriages on the very last day of 1884 had turned out to have been a rather impetuous action on his part. Sir George was still at Pendell Court in the last week of July 1885, taking his turn at hosting the annual Bletchingley and Nutfield Cottage Garden Society. He was also still there in the last week of October to welcome Princess Louise, one of Queen Victoria's daughters, and her husband Lord Lorne.

There were rumours, however, that it wasn't a purely social call, but they had expressed an interest in purchasing the house. But in November 1885 Sir George still hadn't left: he was on the platform at a noisy meeting of the Conservative Party just down the road from Pendell Court in the village of Nutfield.

Early in 1886 Sir George did finally leave England and went to live for a while in Italy. It is not clear whether Miss Sams accompanied him, but it seems likely that she did. In her evidence at the infamous libel case of 1893 Catherine Aberdeen testified that she had been in the service of the Macleays for some seven or eight years.

The appointment, or promotion, of Frank Ross to be Green's replacement also makes it clear that, wherever he was planning to live, Sir George had decided that the gardens should continue to operate at the highest level. Ross was another highly accomplished horticulturist who, until he joined the garden staff at Pendell Court in 1883, had been working at Kew. It is impossible to tell whether he had already been earmarked as Green's successor, or whether his presence at Pendell Court was simply fortuitous.

By the summer of 1887 Sir George had returned, appearing once again as a prominent figure in English Society and playing the part of Lord of the Manor to the full. It was his contribution of £50 that made possible the gargantuan scale of the Bletchingley Feast in honour of Queen Victoria's Golden Jubilee – a meal that required over 1000lbs of beef, 700 cabbages and 7cwt of potatoes. Later that year, in September, both he and Miss Sams are recorded as visitors to the fashionable Alexandra Hotel, Hastings. By then, of course, Charles Green had been dead for almost a year.

In the gardens too, for some time at least, it seemed as if nothing had changed. In 1886 Frank Ross was mentioned approvingly in what proved to be *The Gardener's Chronicle's* last full-length article on Macleay's garden. Ross was cited as an expert on the cultivation of *Denobrium* in the Orchid House. In the same year, more mundanely, he put an advert in the *Surrey Mirror:*

'WOMAN *wanted for Garden Work (young and brought up on a farm preferred). – Apply between nine and ten o'clock in the morning at The Gardens, Pendell Court, Bletchingley.*'

The Gardeners' Chronicle appreciated Ross's expertise in other areas of horticulture too, as in December 1888 they published an article by him on the cultivation of *Aralia*. In the same year Ross used the *Surrey Mirror* to try and sell a cow he owned. However, on the death of Sir George in 1891 his connection with Pendell Court ended abruptly. His successor, the otherwise anonymous Edward Duncan, was left to preside over the sad task of selling off '*....one of the richest private collections of plants in Europe.*' .

For Frank Ross it was just one of those things that happened to servants. He accepted it stoically as an employee was expected to, and set himself up as a nurseryman in nearby Merstham. His status amongst his peers didn't diminish; through the early 1890s he served, as Green had done, as a member of the Royal Horticultural Society's Floral Committee.

Frank Ross makes his final appearance in the story of Pendell Court in January 1892. He was called as a witness in a criminal case brought before Godstone magistrates. Although Ross had given up working in the gardens in August 1891, he still lived nearby, and the court proceedings give an indication of how quickly what had once been a famously well-ordered garden was now slipping into a more chaotic state.

The magistrates dealt first with Thomas Watson who, while working as a bricklayer at Pendell Court, had spotted Ross's ice skates on a windowsill and stolen them. He was fined £4. More serious was the conduct of his friend, Samuel Wright, who had managed over a period of time to remove from Pendell Court gardens: a saw, a hatchet, a number of lily bulbs, two bundles of wire netting, a mat, two watering cans and a garden trowel. He was sentenced to six months hard labour.

Pendell Court was bought from Macleay's executors in 1893 by Mr. W.A. Bell who had made his fortune in America. A year later The *Gardeners' Chronicle* reported hopefully:

'The beautiful and, in some respects, unique garden formed at Pendell Court, near Bletchingley, by the late Sir George Macleay, has, we learn, fallen into good hands, Mr W.A. Bell, the present proprietor, being in full sympathy with that style of horticulture for which Pendell Court became famous, and which was so successfully managed, first by the late clever Mr. Green, and afterwards by

the no less clever Mr. Frank Ross. The garden was so full of interesting plants both tender and hardy, that, despite the stripping it received after Sir George's death, it is still well furnished with all kinds of herbaceous plants and shrubs, some parts of it looking as though they had never been interfered with…we note with satisfaction Mr. Bell's intention to run Pendell Court Gardens on the old lines.'

But it was not to be. For the Bells, Pendell Court simply became a genuine family home at the heart of a sporting estate with pleasant, well-kept, gardens that had no horticultural pretentions at all. As was the case with many large Edwardian establishments the lack of manpower during the 1914-18 war caused an irreversible decline in the upkeep of the grounds. A photograph from that time shows the two Incense Cedars that dominated the front of the house bedraggled and unpruned and the front lawn apparently cut for hay.

Emily Green's life had been a difficult one. Head Gardeners weren't particularly well paid and before and after her marriage to Charles, Emily appears to have taken responsibility for all the domestic duties: cleaning, cooking, washing, ironing, mending, shopping, and for bringing up her step-daughter. There is no record of the Greens ever employing a domestic servant.

Emily lived for another 33 years after her husband's death. In 1911, aged 84, she was living by herself in one room in Reigate, earning her living as a needlewoman. Her firm, bold, signature on the census form shows no signs of advancing age. She died in 1919, the same year as Lady Augusta Macleay, but in very different circumstances.

Charles Green's daughter Lucy had married a local ironmonger, James George Batchelor, in 1876. They lived the rest of their lives next door to the shop, in a little two-up, two-down, terraced cottage, number 33 Holmesdale Road in Reigate. They had eight children.

The fate of one of Lucy's sons, Harry, is a poignant symbol of the changes that engulfed the world his grandfather had known. Aged 21, as Private H. Batchelor, no. 50993. serving with the 18th Bttn. The Manchester Regiment, he was killed in action on the first day of the Third Battle of Ypres, more commonly known now as Passchendaele. He has no known grave.

By the same date Hillfield House in Reigate had

become Hillfield Hospital for convalescent soldiers. Borrer's house, along with its garden, at Barrow Hill in Henfield retained much more of its shape and original content until it was commandeered by the Army in the Second World War when it suffered severe damage. By the 1960s it had disappeared under a new housing estate.

The outbreak of war again in 1939 marked the end of Pendell Court as a country estate. Its further decline was arrested only by its purchase in 1961, from an order of nuns, by Christopher and Dudley Bull, preparatory school proprietors. They found little evidence, or use, for what had once made it famous.

'...a playground was planned to the north, where an orchard lay...derelict greenhouses were excavated for a swimming pool. The lawns in front of the house, including a paddock, were merged with some tree-felling and levelling to make a cricket ground.'

❀   ❀   ❀

Precisely why Sir George invested so heavily in the gardens at Pendell Court remains unclear. He published nothing on any of his scientific or horticultural interests. Despite his connections with leading scientific associations and authorities of the day, and his success and experience of Australian agriculture, there is no evidence that Macleay ever thought of developing his interest in growing southern hemisphere plants in northern hemisphere conditions for any commercial or altruistic reasons.

Gardening on a grand scale was fashionable at the end of the 19th century. Many of the other impressive gardens of the period were cultivated to give their owners an enviable status in society. There are other, different, ways for Pendell Court to be defined. As well as being a suitable adjunct to his knighthood, Macleay's gardens can be seen as a natural extension of the pioneering work carried out by his father in Australia, a vibrant testimony to the qualities of the latest thinking on garden aesthetics, a test bed for serious scientific investigations, and a dazzling display of the heights expert horticulturalists could reach when freed of financial constraints. Equally, the gardens can also be thought of as an expensive hobby in which he wished to indulge himself for as long as it amused him.

If the latter is true then he was simply keeping step with his fellows as they raced their yachts, shot innumerable pheasants, collected stamps, bred exotic poultry, climbed in the Alps and played baccarat with princes. If this was the rationale behind the gardens at Pendell Court it might help to explain why Sir George made no provision for their future.

Another argument is that this lack of planning demonstrated how clearly Macleay understood that the essence of all gardens is their impermanence. They are for the present only, and can never be monuments for their makers. Macleay's father, brother and cousin looked deeply into the natural world hoping, as they amassed their huge collections, to find patterns and order – a guide to understanding the meaning of life on Earth. George lived for the moment, enjoyed it, and looked no further.

Charles Green is a complex, haunting character. He overcame the disadvantages of his birth, education and background to develop an extraordinary understanding of the gardening *zeitgeist* of the late 19th century. His ability to match this with the mastery of the scientific, horticultural and management skills required to make the theories of others a physical reality, mark him out as an exceptional figure in any age.

What is most appealing about Green is his

humility. Throughout his working life he waits to see what a new plant will do; he gives it time to grow and mature before he decides how best to use it. He creates environments that suit his plants, and never forces them into situations where they cannot flourish. He displays them with a sensitivity as to their individual characteristics. He is upset when the plants in his care fail to prosper. He loves them for their beauty and their differences. Most of all he understands that gardening is not simply a science, but a delicate balance between art, nature and craft.

What makes the tragedy of his death heartbreaking is that the serenity that served him so well as a gardener deserted him at the end. His retreat from the astonishingly vibrant gardens he had created at Pendell Court to die drunk in the small, dark, terraced house in Reigate, becomes almost symbolic in its finality.

'They looking back, all th' Eastern side beheld
Of Paradise, so late their happy seat...
The World was all before them, where to choose
Their place of rest, and Providence their guide:
They hand in hand with wandering steps and slow,
Through Eden took their solitary way.'

SOURCES

Permission to use the letters of Charles Green was generously granted by the State Library of New South Wales. The letters form part of the MacArthur Family Papers 1789-1930 vol. 58, call numbers A2954, microfilm CY 2256.

Permission to use the portrait by Hubert Herkomer of Sir George Macleay was generously granted by the Mitchell Library, State Library of New South Wales digital order number a928002.

Permission to reproduce the photograph of Charles Green was generously granted by the Surrey History Centre. Albumen Print 63mmx104mm. Ref: 3770/1

The Gardeners Chronicle and *The Garden* can be read online, for free, courtesy of the Biodiversity Library at biodiversitylibrary.org

The Australian newspaper archive can be accessed, for free, via trove.nla.gov.au/newspaper

UK records of births, marriages, deaths, wills, military service etc were accessed via ancestry.co.uk

British newspapers were accessed via britishnewspaperarchive.co.uk

Some of the material printed here has appeared before, in a much abbreviated form, in *Hortus* and *The Journal of Garden History*.

From 2005 to 2013 the author worked with the pupils of The Hawthorns School, which now occupies the site, to try and recover and understand what still remained of the gardens at Pendell Court.

handforged99@hotmail.com

Lightning Source UK Ltd.
Milton Keynes UK
UKOW01n1221070416

271757UK00001B/2/P

9 781909 465459